Chronicles of the Pig & Other Delusions

Other Poetry by Edward Bruce Bynum:

The Dreaming Skull
Godzilla: His Life and Visions

Chronicles of the Pig
& Other Delusions

Poems by
Edward Bruce Bynum

LOTUS PRESS

Detroit

First Edition
First Printing

International Standard Book Number 978-0-9797509-2-2
Library of Congress Control Number 2009907716

Printed and manufactured in the United States of America

Grateful acknowledgment is made to *Stories from the Other Side* (5th ed.) in which "Rhapsody in Two" first appeared and to *The Dreaming Skull* which first published "Impressions." Our gratitude also to Dr. Jackson L. Davis, III, heir of Malvia Roberts, for permission to use a reproduction of her painting, "Oh, Stand the Storm," for the front cover of this book.

Lotus Press, Inc.
"Flower of a New Nile"
Post Office Box 21607
Detroit, Michigan 48221
www.lotuspress.org

This book is livicated to
William Boylin and Ernest Stableford,
two wise gentlemen from Verona
who know better than this.

Contents

I

Chronicles of the Pig: An Allegory of the Osiris

(Optional: Read aloud accompanied by a drum background)

I

The sow's belly heaves
And spits out my form; a
Dead ear, jellysmooth skin, bristlethick
With hair, odd vowels gushing from the neck.
Into this holy day I am born.

The barnyard is babbling, a maze full
Of scratches, hens' clucks, corn.
A blue Dodge rusts near the orchard
Gate. Cows come near on the therapeutic plantation.
Relatives in the East had told them

About this event. Great stars
Splash in the heavens, shepherds get stoned.
It gets so clear at night
Mountains in the distance pile up against each other,
Swelling eternity. Suddenly, a disturbing spiritual accident.

They consult the Dark Book hidden
Six hundred years ago
In a vault, its pages musty,
Crumbling like cake. Still
They manage to read the difficult parts.

It seems I was set for a different delivery.
The virgin mother was still in labor,

Joseph was crying. Three
Wise men were obscenely joking. Later all over Judea
Young boys are bayoneted.

They shut the Book. Scatter
Its ashes. Excise the memory of it.
"What are we to do? Animists, star worshipers,
Soldiers of the past had a name
For this. We shall call him Conchis."

II

"Conchis fucked his way through childhood."
Yes, I heard them say so
After church one Easter in a particularly
Difficult year. It was the winter
They repossessed my father's artificial heart.

He had stopped the payments months
Earlier in order to help out with
The national debt. Washington
Appreciated it; they sent green
Form letters over and over.

My mother's being a nurse is no
Accident. She knows the secret, chose to worship
In the birth place delivery room. When stillborn hearts
Pass her way
They crowd the skies of limbo.

My hair grew thickly, my pig
Thighs receded. Even the nose folded
Up and did its part to take on
The human address. Since my birth
Polite people have not mentioned it.

I awake suddenly in the electric
Morning, sun firing color through
Me like an autumn leaf. For no
Earthly reason I dream of botulism.
Nights I heat by the wood stove.

III

Romances are my specialty. I've mounted
Stray dogs, odd chickens, an occasional
Goat. My childhood had noises
In the barnyard, whistles.
The corn oceaned in before winter.

From small animals I went to machines.
I invented marijuana
Several times over. Clouds belched dwarfs
And grills of Edsels across the brain's hemispheres
Always turning from the left.

A priest once confessed I was
Certifiably insane. I overheard him at a cocktail
Party at the Vatican one summer.
He also mentioned I masturbated.
I was terrified, ran. I stole a taxi.

The whole episode was later featured
In *Time* magazine. He had
Confused me with an escaped Vedic
Priest. He said I had had
A timeless love affair with Teilhard de Chardin.

By late March my capacity was legend.
Whole tribes of women swore
They had slept with me. Stanford University
Went experimental with my blood type. I filled
Ashtrays with anxiety, sweat.

Once I made love twelve times
With a one-armed dead movie star. It was late
Summer, quiet; the tree frogs were
On strike. She came up to me in a
Nun's outfit. Then she dropped the robes, the beads, the cross.

IV

At thirty-two Conchis discovered hemorrhoids
And ontology. His Self kept going
Back and forth from him to me to I.
Several times in dissociated states
His voices swelled into family arguments.

From which time should he speak?
From now, from I, from the center
Of the Self? From the periphery,
The wider vision of his being? Or from
Me, the body, the continuum through space?

6

He sees Mount Kenya fill with sad heroes and the Orisha.
The grandfather of all this
Did snuff in a rocking chair and inherited
A millennium. Parts of the Self reflect back
Through him, mirrors into mirrors receding.

But just where was the Being
In all of this? He looked at his arm,
Saw aging veins; the face he owned
Had gray marbled through hair.
The excess fat of thirty years

Suddenly thickened around his heart. He did
Not remember his past, was uncanny
At knowing his future. His Being
Eluded him each time he happened upon it.
Through each generation, though, his ears

Were the same. His clothes flickered on/off/on
Like an old newsreel at the picture show. He had visions
Of the Fox Trot, Bessie Smith and the hammers
Of Chicago. He dreamed he saw
His great-great-grandfather born as a slave.

Then the root of the Self escaped
Him again. Each time his hunger
Annihilated the vision. Then suddenly
He surrendered the struggle, embraced telepathy.
His hands grew younger by the moment.

Later he studied psychokinesis,
The subtle gravity of the occipital lobes.
What he learned was what he
Already knew about a flower
And so laughed his way to Hollywood,

77 Sunset Strip. He wrote a primer
On parapsychology, breathed into it
His testament. The mescaline that questioned
His nervous system read the book.
Leopard fetishes and formulas leapt

From the brain, ratifying intuition
Outside of time. During life we look outward,
During death we look in; children,
Seaweed, Ho Chi Minh. Patterns
And parities localized in him.

Then slowly he remembered he had always been.

V

At 53 Conchis realized God was bored
With him. He received no messages
During sleep. Days became nuisances
Like dog shit. Fields went early brown

To winter. The stellar establishment of planets,
Tides and the age of trees hardened him
Into hickory. Then the back of his
Language broke. Conchis drilled into an eerier canyon.

8

He learned to decipher the markings
In trees. Streetcars loaded with bacteria
And screams entered his asylum of voices.
His medical director interned at Auschwitz.

The guards were all children; the therapists
Ate mushrooms, wore green hats.
The admissions unit was decorated wall
To wall with color television sets. He was on

The Managed Care Group Plan, sponsored by Death House
And Casualty, Inc. Sessions began
Ritually at 8 o'clock. The first
Month he dreamed repeatedly of Medusa

And the loosened snakes of Africa
Running in blood down the continent.
Faces turned salt and stone
Habitually in his presence. His therapist

Was an ex-KGB sergeant. His mane flew
Over cities and temples to the dead.
Dust gathered in his mouth. Conchis
Decided to *abandon* his body.

He fell asleep with a revolver in his
Hand. Freeways grew on his inner landscape.
He fell in love with suicide and his father.
Four brothers ate bitters for breakfast.

Then the deeper dream *outside* his body
Widened by faces. Strong faces,
Emergency faces, faces that wait
At the end of trolley lines. Heroes

And horses spleened through the meadows,
The rivers fed like arteries.
He had reached escape velocity.
He had evacuated the skull.

Bit by bit he entered the wild zoo
Of his kin. Mad cousins, hospitalized aunts
Ruddered through his memory's swamp.
Lynching and astrology happened here.

The backwater priest with amulets
Praised the violence of owls,
The necessity in bone. Conchis watched.
Midnight increased the sky, stars blithered.

Motorcycle Nazis inhabited the roads. He
Saw them as he rose roof over roof,
The dreamscapes of villages,
The Swiss genius for snow.

Night after night he returned
To this. Days hurt him when
They were too long. He became
Fixated on his heartbeat. Hours

Swelled in the migraine vein. Sleep
Brought the right mix of death, dream
And desire. He eluded schizophrenia,
Went farther.

He studied the delusions of Santa Claus,
The crude motivations of the bat.
A federal grand jury became his conscience
The 83rd year into his birth.

By then forms of spiritual cancer had become
Common. The unabridged memory
Wreaked havoc with the heart. Calcium
Gathered at the nodules.

Then for two decades nightly he had the same
Dream about himself. In the dream
He rose, green flame and cape
Surrounding the body,

The pouch where the soul warms.
Beelzebub the devil asked him for a date.
They met over lunch, exchanged
Maps and Tarot cards in a language of ancient races, then ran

To a computer, got lost in its virtual spaces.
Green smoke covered everything. There
Was violence in the air and lung.
Out of a cloud a revolver came.

God put it into his hand.
Just before he pulled the trigger, his mother
Appeared, snorted into the air.
Nightmare disappeared, he met the mornings wet.

VI

By age 103 Conchis was diseased.
The headstone honed in granite
Above him ate into the winds of the planet.

Desiccated, he had left his entrails
Under rock. He walked where the dervish
Inhabit. Scenes ganged in on him.

Knives and flags exercised on the road.
Through thickness and greenhood
He moved in a subtle language

Known to the starling and orchid.
Dead in one level of his mind,
Splash young in another.

Spontaneously he remembered his last
Birth. How everything got confused, panicked,
The shepherds wanting their money back.

Conchis wandered into the old plantation
Again. Everything had changed.
The barnyard was turned

Into a blue apartment complex.
Everyone's face had fewer lines.
Gravel turned into asphalt

Had replaced the dense earth
They extracted worms from.
A magician and voyeur spotted

Him first. Smiles oceaned in.
He had completed the initial task.
After the first conscious death, the rest are easy.

Conchis began his own rowing toward God.
Sexton had dropped off
Where the agony ended. Lowell took

A stroke, then a successful heart attack.
Dylan Thomas vomited his last verse
Into a gutter of blood and alcohol.

Yet Aimé Césaire retook his island;
Walcott, near death, ate
Flames and words.

All the poets beyond flesh
Watch the winter sky, snowflakes fall
Like injured angels in the wars for Heaven.

Conchis met them all along the path.
One had holed up on an island
Of salt, built an altar,

Became sexual with witches.
Another was condemned back to birth.
Still another moved on quicksand,

Used a green blade for a sail.
They were coming nearer.
Other signs pointed the way.

There were saints on crosses,
Ruined monks, flaming Buddhists
Struggling in the mud. There were

Taoists, Hare Krishnas, hot Deists
And holy Catholics. There were pantheists, Orunmilists,
And a renegade cousin of Zarathrustra.

Conchis kept on walking, rowing;
Conchis kept on awakening toward God.
His eyes could no longer distinguish.

His arms became useless, heavy.
The last memory of body form
Fell out from beneath him.

Movement was known by intensity, duration.
He spilled on the beach of creation.
Love is gravity—

The eerie frequency
Of psi and motivation, an algorithmic confluence
Of the intimacy and intensity between us.

Families get it most, then lovers and friends,
Rarely strangers. We drift through
Each other's dreams, dimly take notice.

Conchis knew the syntax and moment
Of grief. Then he knew surrender,
The many apples of Boston.

VII

Chokeberries, hair, the green hysteria
Of seaweed, thin snow, voices,

Academies of the past. He seeped
Like a grandfather into God's left ear.

He heard the ongoing bark
Of tears, the future rifts of mother, daughter.

He could easily be in a grapefruit,
A checkbook. His anatomy was thought.

He opened moments and lives like a pomegranate,
Seeds held shoulder to seed. Red beads

Pilled out, reality kept eluding form.
He soon *felt* the Buddha, Christ,

Innumerable smaller prophets. They
Were seated in a circle, attendant

Crosses, robes and oracles. A fountain
Of light gesticulated in the middle.

He came to the Maya of voices,
Theories. Forms, alphabets,

The constructs of memory
Giving way slowly to what he could not speak.

Silence opened, fell into him,
An elevator plunging innumerable flights.

He forgot he had ever been born.
Beyond in or out, beyond the pulse in the thigh,

He *felt* of trees, of the *intention* of roses, heard
In the silver birch of autumn; *All of That Am I.*

II

Meditations at Midlife While Sitting in the Dark

I

I sat on the back porch one summer remembering
That energy and consciousness are eternal.
So when death collapses love

Around the heart and the bright delusion of individuality holds
      reality
Like an iron instrument,
I cough up the first two centuries of my youth,

Offer them to the deciphering wind,
Catch whatever leaves fall over my face
Like a burial mound or some other testament.

Among the eroticism of roses
My injured dreams look this way and that,
Hoping for a new author. My hands sweat.

I have dark ruminations about the prostate and testicles.
I repair memories of the pyramids I once built,
Then walked through in Egypt and early Mexico.

Habitually I sacrifice everything I invent.
This is why insects attack me,
Why squirrels and green snakes only inhabit

The lower lawns of the property I live
And breathe on with my wife and two sons
Destined to live beyond me.

Infested with dreams I have been seduced by wine,
Green flowers, the ambush of lilac
On a moon flooded night. Amid love and debris

I have been strong enough to punish fear, send appetite
Back to the belly of desire where fish,
Fable, all the ports of dim memory

Breed and fornicate before accepting
The fashionable gospel of recovery.
This snapshot, this splinter of victory

Spirals me into the word's snare, a whirlpool of feeling.
The moon hunts the darkness. I am an invisible corpse,
A cemetery wanderer. Necromancer in the city of the dead,

I walk among those still clinging to their sensations on the
                astral planes
While the body-idea each year dissolves
Like the fog over the mouth

Of a great valley in the morning. The sun
Is a pagan ritual, the eyes are altars.
In the blood a hidden divinity

Delights in pain and the motive for release.
All this is happening in a fragment
Of the Milky Way, in a tissue of spacetime,

In an instant between the games of inexpressible owls
Before they swoop down, devour my gullet,
Heal the tear in eternity my voice has crept through.

II

In the terrifying contraction of a god
I have taken root, become a naked disciple of fire, moisture
          and morsels of earth.
I worship the sea breeze, the kelp, the garbage,

The torn bits of wisdom
Gulls confirm when they pick through
The bodies that have exhausted their element.

Ashes to ashes and gold to bankers,
The jaguar roams the jungle even after the plummet serpent.
A close autopsy of the heart reveals

The bilingual edition of our fate in the body.
Part of us goes to sunrise and sex, to music,
Anatomy and the rapture of lovers

When the seacoast is at its best. This leads
To flowers, to birds, to rivers we fall in
Like sweet vegetables in a broth.

Its faith is colored green
And it transcends the alphabet. It is wished
To you at weddings, murmured over your casket.

Butterflies believe in it, holding
In their glands the chemistry of their metamorphosis.
The other language is more subtle suggesting

A letter that may never be opened.
The body goes there only following the mind
Lost in a swoon. It has no hands.

Tongues stick to its eyes; a barracuda is constantly
Eating at its throat. You leave the body
Like a winter coat whenever you can,

Pierce this new land. Entering it fully,
You are absolved of understanding; witnesses
Spring from the pores of the skin.

Every lie you have ever told
Unfolds a world of injured creation.
Then you are abandoned

By everything but light.
The animals of terra firma marvel and exclaim
At your discarded garments.

III

The heart is a wicked bird over a thousand years old.
On its wings I fly
Through the mouth of dead poets from an unknown country,

Through cinnabar mountains, through temples of ash.
I encounter tribes of lost soldiers,
Forgotten dialects, partly hewn sculptures

From ancient stones. The eye is a linguist
Looking closely at the writings, scouring the scriptures,
The scattered rocks. They tell of my history long before I am
        born.

I am to meet a desert angel,
Partially imprisoned in the flesh, who has hair, has teeth,
Who knows the Spice Islands in the seas of grief.

I am to catch her, wed her,
Fill her hips with boys and souls.
My body will become a holy savage

Full of wisdom, semen and blood.
A crocodile shifts somewhere between my shoulders.
On the hypotenuse stretched between clarity and insight

I am invaded by a disturbing theme. Any minute my heart
        could implode,
The swarm of evil birds it releases
Become the prophecy of swans above a brilliant lake.

A Brief Explanation About Death

I

A dark bird, intolerant and religious,
Flew up from a black canyon screaming,
"Why is there death?" Around him

Eels, onions and interns lay open,
Praying to the sun in the red wake of the morning.
Corpses of trees turned to stone,

Water took on the energy of hands.
The labia majora of everything went holy;
A vestigial darkness hung out in the west.

Suddenly, suddenly like a gorgeous phoenix,
The fiery sky stopped its circulations,
The sea waves froze in their space.

Something beautiful was happening.
Dismembered children walked out of a mirror,
Spread a picnic on the lawn

Below his feet. Between apples and lemonade
They confessed elaborate secrets,
Made his dry tongue retract in its hold

Like a switchblade. When their eyes opened
Only angels came out; small fish left
The lakes for the new gospel they heard.

Nightingales, pigeons, peregrine falcons on the verge of
    extinction
Came from the forest to hear
The brutal symphony the dark bird

Wanted to relate. He was not alone.
Looking to the left, a small limegreen snake
Revealed a spiritual, family mystery.

A garnet eye, spine of edible bone,
It attended the preacher bird
As he ascended the animal throne.

From the edited speech,
In tablets and testosterone
Came a song about honey beer, ginger,

The opulence of rice, even foam, celestial jazz,
And warm hormones like melatonin that regulate sleep
Until finally, like a black hand

Coming out a sea of milk and ice,
The foreign blood was made to speak
On death, delusion and animal sacrifice.

II

An ancient law holds that,
By sex and death, the species unfolds,
Rocks fall into rivers, pigs swill and bite.

Once in a dream the dark bird was swallowed whole
By a great tuna,
Digested slowly, then fully excreted,

Both feathers and feet, on the shore
Of a blue and indigo universe.
Pelicans with three eyes and innumerable feet

Watched his subtle moves. Leaves
And seaweed of deeper and deeper green
Attached themselves to his half broken beak.

He crushed a spider; it jumped back up
Twice its size. He cut a flower;
Its smell grew more intense. He grabbed

A tree, ripped off a limb;
Its roots unearthed and massaged his bones.
He had come to the land

Where death had no place.
There was multiplication, extravagant division,
Realms and rolls of addition

But no subtraction. Thorns and rainbows
Increased their reactions like tremors
And nerve work in the cosmic belly of a huge beast

That knows no birth while fetuses
Run on the light waves between cannibal black holes
And quasars. Here a race of worms can pilot starships,

An acorn can become a professor.
Insatiable nuns with honey between their hips
Copulate with bees suffusing the sky

With a blue amethyst.
Atheists are over employed and cynics have no groins.
Unborn eyes are prematurely bright

With a brave, unearthly radiance.
Yellow roses in the morning speculate
On the rare possibility of death.

Exhaling pollen like a child's breath,
They crowd together in a vase
On a windowsill that cliffs over a valley

Where several lawns intersect.
Among beetle and praying mantis
Apparently the subject also holds interest.

"So why is there no death, no subtraction,
No loss? We steal from neighboring
Universes, eat time, crush atoms

For energy and nourishment. It would
Be so much easier if we could borrow
The weird eraser of vision and existence."

All the mangoes agreed. So did the turnips,
The elephants, the blue whales and the geese.
An election was held. Death was voted in

By an earthquake and catastrophe. Tragedies mounted,
Pain and electrocution came.
Bullets were no longer hungry

In the guns that burned and entertained.
Order was restored to quartz crystals
And daisies. Death as a dry finger was attached to everything.

Sweat beads and breath were legislated into its tax.

Conversations and Decisions with a Promise

After talking with the mountains and the skies
Beyond them, and the clouds that move through them
Like luminous fish; after consultations

With the eagles, debates with the buzzards,
Enduring the vicious vocabulary of the rats,
I have decided, like the ocean, not to die.

For this spiders and jackals have placed me
Under house arrest. I can have no visitors.
All meals must be inspected; police

Pry open my eyelids if I try to fall asleep.
Despite their intentions, though, I steal
Some relief. When the hidden cameras are off,

I switch places with my shadow. A burlap bag
In the cellar is where the soul is encased.
From here I hear conversations among the moles

On the other side of the wall, in the ground,
Three feet four inches from the water.
They are discussing my case

Like a clinical rarity. Inflamed with jealousy
The head mole suggests chemotherapy,
The intern, wheat germ and brown rice.

29

The charge nurse says a soup of vinegar, red leaves
And lice, while the security chief suggests
A therapeutic kick in the butt.

I am alarmed by their inaccuracy.
No, I will not die, but I will transform.
Share with me the secret verities of the bat,

The longevity of redwoods,
Why a peach feels like sex. If you do,
Then I will further share with you the heart of Osiris,

The eye of Horus, the carbon base
Of the life-current that gesticulates through
Nerve links, ebony, music and the view

That angels have shipwrecked and stranded on our rocky
    planet.

Rhapsody in Two

(For Alyse)

I
I Am Your Witness

Through hair, dandelion and the wave of splendor,
Through meetings, neurosis and promise
I am your witness.

Through memories, men and maniacal horses,
Through the flimsy bones of the sea
I am your witness.

Through scarlet fists of cloud hurling at the sunset,
Through the premonition of swans
I am your witness,

Through cinemas, cicadas and the faith of crocuses,
Through the sweet lust of bees
I am your witness.

Through the belly of suspicion, through
The cockseat of decision, through the vermilion
Wisp of your mouth I am your witness.

Through the vision and blackwing of butterfly
And bat, through the age of heroes beyond silence
I am your witness.

Through childhood incandescence, through
Ropes and repression, through cataracts
In the riverblood of the heart I am your witness.

Through small boys in jeans out fishing for salmon,
Through their father's nightmares of war and famine
I am your witness,

Through the smooth ambition of your knees,
Through kisses, through the earthy heat of your smile
I am your witness.

Through longing and metaphors, through lovers in their
        eighties,
Through campers drifting at night,
Through the sidereal mountains I am your witness.

Through birds and the seasons, through polyglot
Mansions, through the myths of first blood and Eden
I am your witness.

Through the fruit fly's durations, through the habits of
        quasars,
Through compound, integral and differential equations
I am your witness.

Through ruins, fireplaces, through multigenerational
        transformations,
Through the perennial burst of morning
I am your witness.

Through hosts and empires, through the hairs of the gnat,
Through the simplest of victories
I am your witness.

Through stonegate and mirror, through the hospital of
        survivors,
Through the warm breath of your mouth,
I am your witness.

Through the knot of winter into the spasm of spring,
Through the funerals of April
I am your witness.

Through summits and quadrants, through swimsuits and
        sneakers,
Through the autobiography of pain
I am your witness.

Through pleasure boats and ghettos, through the obscenity of
        Hitler,
Through the Connecticut countryside
I am your witness.

Through worms, talismans, through the religion of Being,
Through the specific gravity of your fingernail
I am your witness.

Through harbors, abandoned woods, over the nape of your
Neck, over fields of dandelion circled by innumerable birds,
Over kennels, rest homes, through the marsh and wicked fog,
I am forever bloodstrong your witness.

II
Newsreel Life '50s & '60s: "You Are There"

(Optional: Read aloud to a drum background)

I was there when
The nuclear hips of Elvis Presley
Pulsed and recognized another America.

I was there when Castro fucked with Kennedy and the media
Off the coast of Florida,
Inviting us all to incineration and sudden heat death.

I was there when the troops of Nixon
Murdered through Jackson, Kent State and the meadows of
        Ohio,
Immolating the eyes of college students and adolescents.

I was there when King and Malcolm
Stretched Black liberation through verb and syntax,
Awakening a furious compassion "by any means necessary."

I was there when vampire professors
Preached the new genetics, ethnic destiny,
Amplifying the floating nightmare of racism.

I was there when Buddhist monks in orange robes
Set themselves ablaze in ritual street fires
Brought nightly to newsrooms and our color television sets.

I was there when the coffin count of napalm fires
Dug holes for the cemeteries of America,
Filling them with fresh boys dying somewhere inside the dark
      belly of Asia.

I was there when narcotics,
College and rock and roll swelled with Black music,
Warming, lubricating the groin of America.

I was there when
Appalachian causalities piled up in Washington, D.C.
Ignored, criminalized by the liberal press.

I was there when truth,
Victory and the FBI were repeated
Over and over in the same reactionary phrase.

I was there when Gulf,
Exxon and the multinational corporations
Committed cancer with OPEC and oil on the open seas.

I was there when Rockefeller,
Chase Manhattan and the CIA
Almost bought America and extinguished her soul.

I was there when burning insurrection
In the cauldron of the cities broadcast to the peoples of the
      earth
The sickness, the promise and the transcendence of America.

I was there when flower children,
San Francisco and Scott Mackenzie drifted through
My smoldering adolescence sleeping in the foothills of New
    Hampshire.

I was there when death ate
Eliot, Pound and Plath, pulverizing the American soul into
    pieces,
Then resurrected her in the 5th Dimension, the Age of
    Aquarius.

I was there when everyone realized
Our homes and gardens were thirty minutes from the silos of
    Moscow,
The Russian missile, the reach of the megaton.

I was there among assassins, acid,
Accelerating dark libidos and the westward migration
Of warm-skinned moonlighting and meditating Himalayans.

I was there when living hearts
Were transplanted, spinning satellites spawned,
Formulas unraveled the smile in the whirl of a chromosome.

I heard the rape of Viet Nam,
Saw the burned genitals of Mai Lai,
Smelled Cambodia thickening like excrement in my lungs.

I was there the hour
Vivian Leigh died; Tara's theme played all day,
Marilyn Monroe reported overdosed in the nude.

I was there when hurricanes
Climaxed over palm trees in the Southeast
And weather became the new bloodsport of the evening news.

I was there when Walter Cronkite broadcast
"You are there." I was there in the skeletal fantasy,
In the wax museum, in the frozen passages,

Obscure byways, the promise of "low yield blast."
I was there in the ferris wheel spin of Dallas,
Sexual revolution, the invasion of the Beatles.

I was there in the perpetual transcendence,
Reemerging in the blessed United States of *now*. I was there
In the freeing of our collective, luminous, Afro-spiritual
        bodies.

Stone Valley

(For Donald Tucker and Milton H. Harris)

Where the dogwood blooms blisterous, white
Over red and root-thick soil flowing
In a meadowcup of sunlight we sight

The hill and smoke-colored mushroom grove.
Small wood snaps like bone as we foot
Through the rhododendron spinning

The brook. Fine burnt wood, soot
From past campfires molds over turning
Back into earth, almost without trace.

Near the small pond it spills
Into the waterweed drifting up toward the surface
Serpenting the waves like black eels.

A millennium of trees, silver sliver birch, witch hazel, oak
Circles a field of daisies glowing,
Blazing as a thousand swans lifting

Toward the sun as we approach.
Where the winter wind coughs
In the boning trees under the pin-faced

Stars and circling hawk,
The granite round stone surges
Domed, breaking the contour of the field.

Lichen teethe into the quartz exposure
Feeding on the crystal that holds it together
Like rock jawbone underneath.

The air is heavy and still
Filling the moments before a sacrifice.
Our hearts speed, drill

Blood through our veins to the precise
Cell and neuron breeding
This vision of stars and images

Rushing past and through the seed,
The fire and ganglion of mind. Our ages
Whiten, crack like paint on a house

Unkept, bled by the yearing wind.
Thick, heavy as marble, words couch
In our mouths, our lungs. We blend

Into elements, extend our
Feeling like roots into earth made fever-warm,
Pregnant enough to send

Trees and flowers rushing to us, swarm
In a cauldron of greens, yellows and brown.
A bird's voice breaks in a wave

Slow and free. Rising from the breathing ground
Is swimming up from a deep cave
Cooled by underground springs, tunnels

That vein the hidden organs of the earth.
Everything is more and less than it is.
The sun hatches us in the surprise of birth.

Wreckage Under the Moon

I

Cold mother, distant and exact,
You puncture the sky
Bald, scolding, white as bone.

Hard stars period
The cracked black facing around you
Over wild, sudden trees below.

From this meatbox home of bone and hair
I watch the digital ghost
Of TV commercials push and blare

The vacuum lift and Lysol rag
Of cleaning weekends sucking the dust
And skulls of insects that dived and gagged

On ionized air near the kitchen light,
Then died in orbit around the electron fire.

II

Across the lake, flat and innocent
As a blade, comes the pale violin
Of a sudden light rain, its high, thin

Voice leeching on the nerves.
Cold and dreamcrossed, I start
Picking the hair and wax from my ear

This heart-thickened year plunging through
My wilderness of sticks and memory
Like a snowfisted wind.

Tight and dry as a mummy, I stiffen
In this sweatercloth clinging, shocking
My body, ghosting this house.

There is little heat, breath burns
Clear and warm, oxygen fires in the chest.

III

The dish hour works me near the sink.
After pots and glass I dry a knife
That could break the gyre of flesh and dream.

Falling backward into the archetypes
I would take my place with the destiny of fire,
Air, formless and free,

Without obligations, guiltless as rain.
The TV needles its vision into my brain.

On Writing Again After Long Silence

My friend's cancer was photographed
In hues of black and white, caught, framed in galley views,
Then hung in the museum of his medical chart.

The same hues link this winter sky
In the first month's ice-boned weather. I can't explain why
    this
And so many other things today feel untogether.

I've found the key again to the memory vault
Where secrets rot like lepers' fingers.
Days are infused with the psychosomatic.

Beaconing out in a river of meaning and event,
Quarreling with the suicide's target,
I swallow a spoon of melody

With fear as I watch the trucks at my window
Going by like bright red fish.
A cool tongue of wind visits

The window, the panes ooze, hiss
Like snakes moving toward me over grass. This crook in my
    neck
Is from too little sleep, the drifting

Depressive wreckage of years, bloodless hours
Spent over words and ideas while
Sperm nearly dreamed themselves out of existence.

Cars insect on the horizon
Just outside my present view. Oh, there's
Nothing so startling as the breakthrough

Into the present. Streetlights hang
Like thin one-armed strangers hoisted
Above an audience of signs.

Police sirens sting the night with thieves,
Appetites, addictive appointments. My jade plant
Listens to all this with thick, rubbery ears,

Its silence, deeper than metaphor
Or rhyme. I emulate it, envy its courage.
A cracked egg leaks

Its yoke, a collapsing eye into the morning's
Frying oil and skillet, but does not disturb my mind's earth-
        bound vision.
Sunlight seeps into its veins as I listen.

My spider plant wrings in nettles
Of green, splinter roots tumbling upward, then down
Into the bay of the air over the sink

Gagged and throated with last night's dishes.
The easy formulas are obsolete, out of reach.
Working my blood now for these lines.

III

Nerve Harmonies and Blood: A Cycle of Lovewords
(Spring 1973-1974)

Impressions

Rhythms navigate you.
Nerve quick, poured light
Distilled from the mirror's quiet,

You know the innerspace between touch
And perception, let the inconceivable
Punctuate you.

Subtlety dialects your voice
Beyond the tone of your apprehensions;
Unintended movements even more express.

Each day gentles with your arrival.

Woodpond Sketch

I

Stump guarded and wet,
The brackish shore diamonds with sand bits
And mica, the bog water thickens

Like a blinded eye. Fever fed days pulse
And speed my sex and heart, cataract my will,
Stream out like dream and blood

Burst from an opened vein. O sun
Blasting down the blue volley of sky,
My need confronts me like an element.

II

Your face, smooth as stone
Under these waters, bells up, pitching
The current off on one direction.

Thin and pure as rare ore, the air
Swims above us curing itself.
Silence holds us in parentheses.

Dreamvoices

I

We made love the first spring morning
Of the year when the bloodfever
And body's will surged through us

Like a vernal rain. By gentle intuition,
Sometimes with your eyes, you broke
The code of wounds I carried

These 25 years
Like a fishbone caught in the throat.
Your hands, hair, soul and flesh pulse

In a marriage of excellence and chance.
Hidden creature of fire and nerve,
Moonlight roots in your blood.

II

Your face, sculptured
As a mountain brookstone, smooth
With eyes near seagreen

And distant as millennia, dreams
Like a Picasso nude in sleep.
When I hold you

Blood betrays my soul's need to ignite,
Burst rainbows and minute stars
That swim out of carnival fireworks.

When we love it is the first
Sea again, storm-struck and innocent,
The heart's first need and where all visions meet.

III

This dim-voiced love plummets with my blood
Down the valley of my bones, the scheme of my flesh,
Waters the air that plunges through my lungs,

Re-explodes in the meat of my heart.
Each nerve-rigged gesture you compose
When caught in the cup of each other's embrace.

I search the archetypes for your name
Born pure as baby blood
Beyond all clarity of air and rain.

Questions

I

What blister and bloom shocked air
First stunned our heat and life-gifted laughter?
Like leaves spilling, seeding the circling wind,

We took in everything about us; colors,
Fevers, voice-ribbed faces
Rose and played upon the nerves of our dreams.

It was only the obvious we did not see.
Blood and imagination drew through us
The bone and viscera, the human rush

Of flesh and breath down the ear of time
To the circling whorl of perception.
Everything said itself through us.

II

What blast of pain and unintended deception
Sent me reeling into this emotional coma?
I barricade myself in verse and silence.

I nightmare at the thought of meeting you,
Your voice still coloring the sidewalks, trees,
Arresting when anything is ambiguous.

III

Is everything true? Does the same rush
Of need sweep through the lust of animals,
Plants, small children conscious

In their pre-Freudian slumber? Is it the same
Death and birth of matter endlessly
Through the rhythmic canal of time and space?

Do my dreams reflect all mind dreaming
Through gravity, woods, elements that flow
In coherence through the universe?

Hate Poem

Excoriating myself for words and feelings
In the cracked silence, the artist in me
Is crass enough to ask, "Enough suffering now

To reach the right word?" My
Self-contempt rivers in a spring thrall
Down the bloodvalley and gullies of my

Soul. I even hate this writing. A
Bad solution, buying myself off with words.
Death is a cleaner, honest exit.

Never been this close before;
The cool razor or knife plunges down,
Uprooting the nerves like worms suddenly

Spaded into the air. Only cowardice
Is friend to this resentment homing
In the body bag of viscera and bone.

Writing Poetry

I

It's a battlefield. Artillery of letters,
Sub keys on the typewriter poised
Before the war hour of word and need.

Some things I know only too well; a steady diet
Of one's self will make anybody ill. I pop
A lifesaver into my mouth, feel

The sugar fire down the throat with ease.
Teeth crush the final burst of solid,
Suck it through the muscled flue.

Every form of love is eventually used.
My heart is in crisis, nettle picked, consumed
With anger beyond any speakable muse.

II

This is no night language of roots and stars,
No regurgitated fantasy seeping up to fill
The stunned hours that swell in the gut

After "our experience." Solid flesh
Has been ripped from my side. My bones
Are gangly, a wind-thumbed chandelier.

The ground under me sinks, rises, sinks again.
Telephone calls pimp my anger.
The whole world hurricanes in my blood.

After Experience

Our sweet thunder is dead.
This summerblood evening out of Lyra
Keels and spreads through my watersleep

Swirling through organs
And metaphors of death. You were autumn,
Always departure, the first bruiseless

Mating of wind and snow. I gouged
At you, sucked energy like a magnet;
I thought even the birds needed you.

Now voices nightmare my peace.
My heart's fist of sinew and nerve
Loosens, retreats after impact.

Part of each day's destination is still you.
I face it, hard and smooth as a fingernail.

IV

To the Holy Feminine in Everyone

To the holy feminine in everyone,
Creatrix, funnel of light and gravity
Unfolding through air, bones and providence.

Autumnal fire and unspeakable rose,
Brains, Cadillacs,
                    Wild invisible deer

Run in your streams navigating the mind,
The mind next to everything with infinity
For its limit.
                    Halleluiah to everybody!

Go beyond verbs to the bright birds
Of the heart. O holy feminine in everyone,
Drink the energy at the base of the spine.

Liberation is here, an order and ontology
Rooted in the cells. The mind rides it
In a science of transcendence curling from the trail

To the intelligent light doming in the skull.
Go from dream to death to bardo
And back. Go to sleep, to waking, to night,

Then day, forgetting yourself each phase
Of the way; many quantum universes,
Mirrors held back to back, the whine

And flap of saline and sac,
Thallasal and creatrix in every actual
And potential act.

II

Let loose the subtle energies from the skull.
Play with vibration, wave.
Watch the moon, watch the thread
Come loose on an old sweater.
Watch the late night cavorting stars
Interlacing the heavens with threads of light,
Each one reflecting, implicating the others.

Watch the subtle theater in the thought.
Hear the loose ticking, the mumble
Behind the spots where you pretend
Not to be me and I accept your counterfeit signature.
Watch the characters take on
Voice after voice. Watch happiness come,
Laughter pass. Watch with death and go eyeless
Into the swallowing dark.

Watch the vast drift in the gray swamp.
Watch the ghost forms emerge from the fearful thoughts.
Watch the angels spin out of noble excesses.
Smell the incarnation of a rose
Or a bat.
            All of this, dream-thought unfolded
From the Source, the everywhere viewpoint, the Knower.

III

So be alive in every city, in every
Dreampost of the world. Wherever there is celebration,
Wherever there is water, nerve.
Learn the crow's prance, the pig's harmonics,
The subtle geometry spruce trees take
When they germinate themselves over graveyards
In patterns between the headstones and spaces.

Be the unfolding in a rose
Washing wave on wave into the beet-red morning.
O holy feminine in everyone,
The voice leaping original in each cell, cloud
And luminous packet. Light upon light
Is your only prophet. Intelligence,
Abundance drink in every pore.

IV

Yes, dogs have a Buddha nature;
Yes, we are all becoming God;
Yes, rain and decay still become April;
Yes, I actually breathed with Walt Whitman;
Yes, you are me on the deepest level;
Yes, the same blood runs through me that ran
        In the first She-one;
Yes, I know my dog is secretly Krishna;
Yes, we are all intelligence, bliss and light.

Ecstatic People Poem #1

I seek *that* for which this is but
A ripple on the void;
I seek *that* that is both the source
And absence of light;
I seek *that* that is the root of "I" arising;
I seek that ecstatic people poem
To *that* beyond ecstasy.

I seek the holy bloodriver that
Dreams life and energy in each day;
I seek *that* in the petalhead of flowers
Stemming out of stool a cow leaves after rain
On a radiant day.

I believe my dog is a small red saint.
Orunmila and the orishas live under my eyelids.
The Upanishads have become the backdrop
Of my dreams. I mumble the Vedas
Unconsciously during the day. For three years now
The Lankavatara sutra has burst
Out of my mouth, uncontrollably,
On paper illuminating the floating nervework of my dreams.

I am a crane seeking
The wild blue fish threading
Under currents, spiking it, eating it alive.
I seek the wild strawberry of sexual intoxication.

I see the invisible energy that binds
My thoughts, drawing me to objects,
Things and events. I know the vortex
To the vital and the way back up.
Sometimes my brain is an ocean of light.

For Alyse at 43

The moon leans down with its invisible hands,
Pulls us along the sand of years
Toward some unknown place.

Every day you display the light
Of the universe and I am held
With more grace than I can understand.

You arrive each day of my life
In the morning, open as flowers sometimes do,
Then close at night and set my heart

Upon the journey of sleep. I curl
Around you in dreams, a lavender scarf,
Fears dissolving like sugar in water,

Like the smell of warm plums in a glass
Of Japanese wine. I do not know
In your 43rd spin around the sun

How many years still grow rich
With your presence. I know only
I am richer when I see your eyes.

Benediction to a Vampire

Sole explorer and watchman of the highway,
Master of the tree's green, acolyte of nerves,
Allow me to awaken in your witness, your name.

I've designed so many mirrors,
Become lost in their reflections, cornering myself,
I am an emptied vein. A white church

In the distance holds up its cross;
The vampire Pope moves from the bushes.
All day I have been reading Berryman's *Love*

& Fame with an adolescent hope of pain
And transformation. Change brutalizes the senses;
Being the poem is the real exchange.

Come sting me in the dark root,
O surviving Angel.
                    The bloodlines are opening into flame . . . .

Praying Mantis

Stick-goddess frozen into place,
Eyes round and immaculate
As a surgeon's mirror. The jaws

Know their precision. She's captured
A cocoon, eats the baby's head, then resumes
The flight towards egg and home. Watching

Her, I eat beef, knucklebones and fingernails,
My own tools before the ripping teeth. I masticate
The poem, then fly on . . . .

Poems

Poets stitch them together: patches of feeling,
Nerve harmonies, weightless memories in their history's flesh,
Cells acrid with images and small deaths.

The mornings redden and bitter like wild berries.
Days collect in a nightmare of Chagall.
Words tighten the sutures, secure as catgut,

A post-mortem taken on experience. Quick!
Bottle them in pages. Pickle them like sweet meats
On a back shelf, delicacies for a winter night.

Psi Dreaming

That night in the mad dream
When the snake beheaded my sister,
You lay shipwrecked

And dreaming against my heart. My breathing
Swelled, broke in thickets
Of cough, annoying

The few images the bloodstream brought.
You moved sideways,
Slipped out of our body lock. Then morning came

Inhabiting everything, a membrane red,
A giant lamprey's mouth. Turning
To me you asked the time,

Hurried to coffee, shower,
Fell into the mirror above the sink, a blue stone into a lake.
Over breakfast you mentioned drowning,

Then a snake you once saw hacked to death by a friend.

Song of the Living Death in Panavision

Trust only the dark echo of your own ego.
Avoid happiness and fusion at all costs.
Segment and iron out each of your dreams.
Memorize your fears and cast a spell
Of lies to cover the inner continent.
Hallucinate death.
Worship these lies.
Fragment any fragment that connects anything
To anything
Until you fall backwards into the pit
Of the heart. Then stand up, walk abreast with death.
Spit out truth until you're frozen like a star.

Aging Woman Watching the Sky

The lilac spumes, breaks
In an ocean around her house
When the wind pulls at the wood frame aching,
Squealing, a trap-tortured mouse.

Blue-bruised and bulging under her skin
The veins twist, course as they extend
Down her legs, mummy wrapped and honed
In nylon. Insight swims. Her face, stretched over bone

Where the hollows cup her eyes,
Turns toward the evening sky
Filling with a kind of wisdom
Not rooted in word or song.

Vermont Park at a Picnic Table

The conifer smell is a nice extension
Into the head, lungs, the muscle-work heart.
Picnic tables go red, then blacken,

The sun ruts on the horizon.
Riding skyward, trees and wind burn into themselves.
Acorns lie on the earth like broken helmets

Scattered after the ritual battles.
The lake dolphins with swimmers.
Water starts in a place higher

Than this, then cuts down into runnels
Where these counter tops bleed.
Great dead trees grab into the stream

Like the bony hands of some vanished giant.
Whitecaps kick with the current
Over granite. Appetite waits in the underpool.

I've Surrendered Many Things to Poetry

I've surrendered many things to poetry.
I've surrendered bats, the wings of fables,
The clock piece with no hands that rings

On my death. I've given up nightmares,
The cult of synonyms, applewine
Dinners with a winter friend.

I've handed over my diaries
That map the skull, brief reports
On necrophilia to journals in the North.

I've abandoned windows, no longer
Take in guests, end everything I feel
With an exclamation point. The smallest

Events have victory over me. In this sense,
And this sense only, I triumph.

Goodbye

Goodbye. I am sealing my address in an envelope
And swallowing it.
Goodbye, I am forgetting my teeth and all my appointments.
So long to Hopalong Cassidy, bottled vitamins,
Naked theories on the origin of the universe.
Arivederci to firm skin and its oils;
Sayonara to gentleness, doctoral degrees;
Auf wiedersehen to memory; adios to stone;
Au revoir to Europe, Asia,
The vast African continent. Goodbye
To radios, the soul and the gunned heart.

About the Author

Edward Bruce Bynum, Ph.D., ABPP, is a psychologist and diplomate in clinical psychology of the American Psychological Association. A recipient of the Abraham Maslow Award of the American Psychological Association, he is currently co-director of psychology intern training and education at the University of Massachusetts Health Services in Amherst, Massachusetts.

Dr. Bynum is the author of five texts in psychology/psychiatry, including: *The Family Unconscious; Families and the Interpretation of Dreams; The Roots of Transcendence; The African Unconscious: Roots of Ancient Mysticism and Modern Psychology;* and the forthcoming *UREAUS: The Science and Mystery of the Shining Light Within Us.*

Dr. Bynum is married and the father of two sons, Ezra and Elijah. He lives with his wife Alyse in suburban Amherst.